How to Talk to People Effectively in Decisive

Unveiling the Europeans Key Secret to Powerful Connection to Win People & Take Over

Dr. Smith Walker

Copyright

2024 Doctor Smith Walker. All intellectual property rights are retained.

Except for brief quotations incorporated in critical reviews and certain other noncommercial uses permitted by copyright law, no part of this book may be reproduce

7d, distributed, or transmitted in any form or by any means, including photocopying, recording, or other electronic or mechanical methods, without the prior written permission of the publisher.

Please contact Dr. Smith Walker for permissions requests.

Disclaimer:

The content in this book is offered only for general informative purposes. The author, publisher, and contributors are not responsible for any loss, injury, or damage experienced as a result of using or using any of the material, advice, or ideas offered in this book, whether directly or indirectly.

While every effort has been made to ensure the accuracy and completeness of the information provided, the author and publisher make no express or implied representations or warranties regarding the completeness, accuracy, reliability, suitability, or availability of the content contained within this book. Any reliance on such material is therefore entirely at your own risk.
This book is not meant to replace expert advice. Readers are advised to seek expert assistance about particular problems or circumstances.

The author's views and opinions are purely his or her own and do not necessarily represent the official stance or position of any other person, organization, employer, or enterprise. When using the ideas in this book, always use your discretion and judgment. This book does not promise any particular results or consequences.
For any additional clarity on the use or dissemination of the material in this book, please contact legal or copyright advisers.

Author Information

Dr. Smith is a renowned author and worldwide best-selling book known for his revolutionary work in the fields of self-improvement and successful communication Dr. Smith has devoted years of study and practical experience to helping people improve their conversational skills, connect honestly, and develop meaningful relationships, with a love for understanding human interaction and communication dynamics.

His intelligent and engaging work has helped numerous people all around the globe handle diverse social situations with confidence, empathy, and efficacy. Dr. Smith's knowledge goes beyond basic conversation skills, diving into the complexities of active listening, body language, emotional intelligence, and assertiveness.

Dr. Smith dedication to assisting others in achieving communication mastery is unshakeable. His earlier best-selling self-help book on successful communication, which received worldwide praise, changed how people approached and engaged in talks. Dr. Smith Walker has also given workshops, seminars, and keynote addresses, offering his expertise to a wide range of groups looking to improve their interpersonal abilities. passion to encouraging people to speak effectively and connect meaningfully demonstrates his commitment to personal development and good transformation.

The Benefit of the Book

➢ Learn basic communication skills that will allow you to express yourself effectively and articulately in a variety of social and professional contexts.

➢ create Meaningful Relationships: Learn how to cultivate real connections, deepen relationships, and create rapport with a variety of people, allowing you to form deeper and more fulfilling ties.

➢ Improve Your Listening Skills: Investigate the power of active listening, nonverbal clues, and compassionate involvement in order to facilitate greater understanding and connection with others.

➢ Learn how to negotiate challenging talks, confrontations, and disagreements with grace, diplomacy, and firmness, resulting in productive conclusions.

➢ Improve your professional communication abilities, such as networking, public speaking, negotiation, and leadership communication, to support career progression and success.

➢ Increase your self-confidence by learning how to speak effectively, convey ideas eloquently, and project confidence in a variety of scenarios.

➢ How Interpret and Use Body Language: Learn the intricacies of body language and nonverbal communication so you may successfully send messages and interpret unspoken hints from others.

➢ Develop Empathy and Emotional Intelligence: Improve your emotional intelligence and empathy, allowing you to connect on a deeper level, comprehend views, and react empathetically to the feelings of others.

➢ Address and overcome typical communication hurdles such as misconceptions, cultural differences, and language difficulties to promote easier relationships.

➢ Practical Exercises, Real-Life Examples, and Actionable ideas: The book includes practical exercises, real-life examples, and actionable ideas that readers can immediately employ in their personal and professional encounters.

How to Use the Book

i. Begin with an Open Mind: Approach the text with an open and receptive mind. Recognize that learning good communication is a continuous process.

ii. Read and Absorb: Thoroughly read the book, soaking in the ideas, approaches, and tactics presented in each chapter. Take your time learning the ideas that have been covered.

iii. Reflect on Personal Scenarios: Consider previous encounters or present communication issues. Relate the principles in the book to real-life scenarios to better grasp their practical relevance.4

iv. Take Notes and Highlight Key Points: While reading, jot down interesting themes, activities, or key takeaways. Highlight portions that speak to you or provide useful advice.

v. Exercises: Actively participate in any exercises or activities specified in the book. These activities are intended to help you practice and reinforce good communication ideas.

vi. Apply skills in Real Life: Use the skills and strategies you've learnt in your regular talks. In your conversations, practice active listening, assertiveness, empathy, and other skills.

vii. Experiment and adapt: Be open to trying out new communication methods. Adapt the tactics to different circumstances and individuals, enabling you to be more flexible in your communication approach. Progress should be evaluated on a regular basis. Take note of any good changes in your communication habits, relationships, or approach to difficult talks.

viii. Revisit and Reinforce: Return to chapters or portions that are especially important to you or that you want to reinforce. Repetition and reinforcement are often used to consolidate new abilities.

ix.   Discuss and Share: Hold talks with friends, coworkers, or peers regarding the themes in the book. Sharing views and experiences may broaden your awareness and open up new possibilities.

x.   Create an Action Plan: Based on the book's principles, create a personal action plan. Set attainable communication objectives and monitor your success over time.

Contents

Introduction

Welcome to an adventure that will change the way you traverse the complex web of human contact. Have you ever been astounded by someone's capacity to connect with everyone, anywhere? Do you want to exert influence via the art of conversation? You're going to discover the keys of effective communication and successful relationships in these pages. Effective communication is more than a talent; it's a superpower that allows you to connect, influence, and prosper in both personal and professional settings. From the boardroom to social events, mastering the art of conversation is essential for making a lasting impression, building important connections, and achieving extraordinary success.

This book is more than just a talking guide; it's a full blueprint meant to help you communicate with ease, influence with elegance, and grasp the nuances of communication. We'll go into the worlds of small chat and big talk, deciphering the complexities of starting conversations and navigating important talks that engage and inspire.

Are you ready to turn meaningless small chat into significant connections? To master the skill of hearing and reacting in a manner that profoundly connects with others? Whether you're an introvert looking for social confidence or a professional looking to improve your networking abilities, the ideas provided in this book will serve as a guide.

We'll delve into the intricacies of social communication, discovering the unspoken principles that govern effective conversations. Each chapter includes practical methods and concrete suggestions targeted to improve your communication skills, from grasping body language indicators to polishing your narrative talents. Communication is the foundation of human contact; it links us, forms our relationships, and drives us forward. We'll dig into the complicated tapestry of successful communication in this book, revealing the keys of making strong connections that resonate deeply and enhance every aspect of your life.

Have you ever struggled to express yourself effectively or connect truly with others? Perhaps you've experienced misconceptions or felt unheard in important talks. You're not alone yourself. Fear not—within these pages, you will learn the strategies to handle these hurdles and emerge as a successful communicator.

This book isn't only about mastering conversation tactics; it's also a guide to making true, lasting relationships that go beyond surface-level conversations. It's about cultivating connections that thrive, whether in the boardroom, across a coffee table, or in the intimacy of personal interactions. You'll learn about the basic ideas that govern effective communication and relationships. We'll look at active listening, assertiveness, empathy, body language, and emotional intelligence along the way. You'll discover how these aspects interact to create the fabric of captivating communication. More importantly, you will learn and practice tactics and exercises that you can instantly utilize in your daily encounters.

Success in relationships, whether personal or professional, is often determined by our capacity to communicate effectively. Whether you want to develop a strong network, negotiate a contract, resolve disagreements gracefully, or just strengthen your relationships with loved ones, the lessons in these chapters will help you. Prepare to discover the secrets that enable people to make a favorable impression, form strong friendships, and leave a lasting impression via the art of conversation. We'll begin on a journey toward communication mastery together, one that promises to enhance your interactions, enrich your relationships, and open doors to personal and professional success.

So, join me on this revolutionary journey into the core of successful communication. It's time to realize your full potential and use the power of communication to create a more rewarding and connected existence.

Let's get started

How to Have a Better Communication with People You Just Met

Speaking with new individuals is difficult since there are so many unknowns. Talking to someone you don't know is a new experience. When compared to talking to your spouse, closest friend, or mother, the unknowns make it difficult and possibly daunting, according to Sandstrom. The other individual may be talking excessively. We could be talking too much. They could go out of business. We could get bored. They can get bored. There might be an awkward quiet. They might be attempting to hit on me.

How you can make yourself more appealing?

We are social creatures. Even difficult interactions are beneficial to our health.

But, despite the uncomfortable pauses, blunders, and unsteady footing, chatting to new people (even total strangers we won't see again) is beneficial to our health. According to studies, even little social contacts (such as conversing with that stranger on the train) might improve mood.

In one study, researchers randomly selected participants as they entered a busy coffee shop in downtown Vancouver, instructing some to attempt to strike up a conversation with the barista and others to be as quick as possible in their coffee fetching. In comparison to the efficient group, the former group reported leaving the coffee shop in a better mood and with a stronger feeling of belonging in their community.

Tricks to Improve Your Conversation Skills with Strangers

Here are some suggestions for approaching someone at a networking event, engaging a friend's pal you've never met before at a party, or chatting pleasantries with a stranger on the elevator (yeah, we went there):

➢ Be brave and less concerned.

Sandstrom suggests being brave and just doing it, even if it is uncomfortable. The person will probably like you more than you think, and you both will probably enjoy it more than you think.

And don't be afraid to approach someone who seems to be different from you.

➢ Be curious.

Ask questions. Is the person wearing a significant item of clothing? Why did they decide to come to the event you're both attending? According to studies, people who ask more questions are better liked by their conversation partners than those who ask less questions.

➤ Don't be afraid to stray from the script.
According to Nightingale, instead of the typical questions (what do you do, where do you live, etc.), ask a question that will make your conversation partner think. Begin with a statement such, "This painting really confuses me" or "I can't believe how crowded the train is today." According to Nightingale, statements are invitations to express one's interest.
Be genuine, whether you're asking a question, answering, or making a comment, she advises.

➤ Pay someone a compliment.
According to Sandstrom, it draws attention to the other person and should make them pleased. She adds that when it comes to our phobias of speaking with strangers, we tend to be in our heads a lot, overthinking what we're doing wrong or what we may do wrong. She argues that concentrating our attention on the other person might help us get through those difficult times.

> ➢ Engage in more conversations with strangers.

According to Sandstrom, the more you have, the more probable it is that you will have constructive discussions. You enhance your ability to ask better questions and provide more intriguing responses. but it's as much confidence that come from just doing it more often," she went on to say.

According to Schroeder, we are terrified of social rejection - that the person will not respond positively or would ignore us. However, research shows that when people are urged to join in a conversation, they are virtually always willing to do so. (According to Schroeder, our fear assumptions fail to account for social politeness norms.)

> ➢ Don't let difficult circumstances get you down.

Based on her personal experience, Sandstrom summarizes the processes of a conversation with a stranger as follows: They initially look at you, as if to ask, "Do I know you?" Then comes the revelation that they have no idea who you are. "Wait, are you some kind of weirdo?" they inquire. Then they see through it all and realize you're just being kind. "You have to be okay with it being awkward for a while," Sandstrom continues. "But if you keep going, hopefully you'll get to that stage where you're having a real conversation."

How you feel about social situations

Use these techniques to become a great conversation partner!

If possible, plan ahead of time.

There are various situations when you know you will meet new people ahead of time, such as:

• Happenings

• Job interviewing

• Get-togethers

• Dates

• Family reunions

Before your meeting, consider the following points:

• What type of relationship do I want to have with this person?

• What topics or inquiries may I launch based on what I know about them?

• Is the setting for our meeting more relaxed or formal?

Did you realize that?
When I go on a first date with someone I met on a dating app, I like to go over their profile for potential conversation topics!

Lower Social Anxiety

There may be a lot of tension and pressure when meeting new people that you won't have anything to say or that you'll be judged for being uncomfortable. The truth is that the vast majority of people feel this way. If you have time before your meeting, try some stress and anxiety management techniques like deep breathing to help you relax.

Did you realize that?

I like box breathing for anxiety relief. Breathe in for six counts, hold for six counts, breathe out for six counts, hold for six more counts, and repeat!

How to Pay Attention to Details

If you can't think of anything to say to someone, look about you for specifics and respond to them. For example, you might talk about:

• Your present environment

• Something distinctive about the person, such as a fantastic piece of clothing

• What you and the other person are doing, such as attending a joint event.

• What brought you two together

Being an engaged listener allows you to pick up on the nuances of what your discussion partner

is saying. Respond with comments and questions that build on what they've already said.
If you're at a loss for words, you may ask them simple questions about themselves or seek their opinion on an issue.

People like it when others show an interest in them!

How to Look for Common Ground

Find out what you have in common with your spouse. As a consequence, everyone who attends will find the discussion more interesting and exciting. These areas of agreement might serve as a starting point for future conversation.

Some things you could have in common are:

• Hobbies

• Sports organizations

• Television shows

Having a preference for or a dislike for the same seasons or types of weather

You may also look at current events to find common ground. Avoid challenging topics, however, until you have a better knowledge of the individual. Someone you're meeting for the first time may feel defensive or put on the spot if you bring up a contentious political issue.

Quiz

What are some topics to avoid while conversing with a potential networking contact at a conference?

➢ The lunch buffet's selections

➢ Their favorite presentation thus far

➢ Speakers with opposite viewpoints

There was an unusual storm on the first day.
Always keep in mind that a discussion takes two individuals.

A conversation is two-way. If someone isn't responding, don't berate yourself. They might have a bad attitude or be an unskilled discussion partner!

However, if you enjoyed your conversation, make sure to contact them later to let them know you had a great time and that you valued what you talked.

Take the Lead
With a little planning and practice, you'll be having excellent first conversations in no time!

Prepare for your next conversation with someone new by doing the following:

➢ Make a note of any similarities you may have.

- ➢ Prepare a few questions to ask them to get the conversation going.

- ➢ Make a strategy to ease your nerves before the meeting.

Ten discussion starters for the State Conversation

You may initiate a conversation on any topic at work as long as it is appropriate for the situation. those with colleagues or business contacts will differ from those with a new friend or acquaintance. Your early efforts may generate a conversation, which may later pay off by supporting you in creating good relationships with coworkers and colleagues. Here are some ideas for workplace discussions:

How to Request information

A good way to start a conversation is to ask the person you want to talk with for information. This is a simple and natural way for connecting with someone. Even if you already know the solution, approaching someone is a good option if you're stuck for ideas.

Pay a compliment

A praise may make someone's day and boost their confidence. You may select any aspect of the person you admire and explain why.

"I really like your hair," said I. "You look good in this cut."

Furthermore, when meeting a prominent someone in your industry for the first time, appreciating their work is a great way to start a conversation.

Make a thoughtful comment

Almost every incident or setting has a beautiful story to tell about it. It may have been the last happy hour at work or a sporting event from the night before. If the person agrees with you, you're on your way to a fascinating conversation.

"Did you see the football game last night?" "I believe our team has finally found their stride."

Introduce yourself

While this is not always suitable, introducing yourself is a simple way to communicate your want to meet someone. For instance, if you've just started a new work and haven't met someone in another department, you may approach them and introduce yourself.

"Hello, my name is Lisa." I'm new to the team and wanted to introduce myself."

In an Interview, How Do You Introduce Yourself?

Offer... or seek... aid

Take advantage of the chance if you find yourself in a position to help someone with whom you want to communicate. Helping others may make you likable and gain their trust, especially if you demonstrate genuine concern.

for example. answer "Do you need a seat?"

Another fantastic way to start a conversation is to ask for help. It works because it makes the other person feel valuable, especially if the support is readily available answer, "Could you tell me where this conference room is located?" or "Could I borrow a pen from you?"

Share a shared experience.

If you want to talk to someone who you know has something in common with you, you may utilize it as a conversation subject. Your common experiences make it easier to get along, facilitating the flow of the conversation and the growth of the relationship.

Collect feedback

Soliciting other people's opinions shows that you value and care about what they have to say. Many people will gladly answer your questions and start a conversation if they are informed about the issue. Consider current concerns while asking input.

"How do you like the coffee from the new cafe?"
"Are they at ease?"

Show real enthusiasm

See if you can naturally bring up a topic about which you know the person is passionate. Passions may get your coworkers talking, and as a consequence, you may learn something new. Remember to keep the conversation light and positive.

"I see [band name] on your T-shirt. Have you seen any of their performances?"

Find out more about them.

People like discussing themselves. Find a topic that enables the person to discuss their interests, family, or experiences.
"That's a great photo of your family on your desk," let's say. "How old are your kids?" disappointing "I heard that you recently took vacation time to visit Hawaii, how was it?"

Make a weather observation

If all else fails, make a weather remark. It's one of the easiest ways to get someone to talk and may lead to a range of topics.

"It's a beautiful day, isn't it?" tell "Can you believe all the snow we're getting?"

Small Talk How to Start a Meaningful Conversation

Using icebreakers to start a conversation
Ice-breaker questions are an entertaining and engaging way to learn more about someone while also prolonging the conversation. Here are 15 icebreakers to consider for your next presentation or meeting:

1. What are you now reading?
2. If you could meet any historical figure, living or dead, who would you choose and why?
3. What was your most recent movie experience? What about it did you find attractive or repulsive?
4. What skill would you acquire if you could learn it in an instant?
5. What is your favorite book?
What's your favorite movie?
7. Tell me about your most memorable trip.
8. What superpower would you want to have?
9. Have you ever checked anything off your bucket list?

10. What would you do with an extra hour in a day if you had 25?

12. Is there someone who has had an impact on your work?

13. What is the most valuable career advice you've ever received?

14 What is your favorite indoor activity?

15. Where would you want to go next?

Getting The Things to Converse

➤ Interrogation and response

Another way to show that you are a good listener is to ask questions. Follow-up questions on what the other person said might assist to widen the conversation. Alternatively, you might question about something you didn't completely understand or are interested in. Again, this shows the person with whom you are chatting that you are really interested in what they have to say.

➤ Identifying common interests and similarities

Throughout a conversation, keep your ears open for similar experiences. Mutual interests may give subjects for discussion and keep the conversation flowing naturally.

Finding common ground may also aid in the development of common ground and a more fulfilling debate. This is a key component of how to keep a conversation flowing.

> ➢ Setting a goal for the discussion

Having a goal in mind for the conversation is typically a good idea, whether you run into a coworker in the supermarket or start up a chat at a networking event.

A well stated aim ensures that the conversation has a purpose and is not unpleasant or uncomfortable.

If you see that the discussion has stalled, you may use your conversation goal to introduce a new topic.

10 Conversation Success Strategies

Do you have any more questions on how to carry on a conversation? Here are some tips to help you be a better speaker in both work and social settings.

➢ Pose a number of queries
Inquiring questions shows that you are interested and paying attention.
Simply let the other person to reply and take the lead. You don't want them to feel interrogated.

➢ Avoid controversies.
Always keep an eye on the situation and the person you're conversing with. Topics that might be considered controversial or improper should be avoided. This might be anything from politics to religion to the agenda of the most recent PTA meeting.

➢ Smile
It is critical to smile while starting a conversation.

Smile at your possible conversation partner before you start talking. This shows your approachability and friendliness.

> ➢ Keep eye contact

Making eye contact shows that you are engaged and immersed in the conversation.

If you keep looking about, the other person will conclude you are either disinterested in what they are saying or are distracted by what they are saying.

> ➢ Give compliments

A compliment is an act of kindness that should never be disregarded. If you complement your conversation partner, they will feel better about themselves. It will also boost the effectiveness of your conversation. Pay attention to what they're saying so you can spot genuine opportunities to praise them.

➢ Seek advice or recommendations

Seek help or advice if you're stuck for conversation starters. This shows that you are attentively listening and value their input.

➢ Avoid becoming excessively pushy.

Pay attention to the flow of the conversation and offer your conversation partner enough opportunity to speak.

You may seem enthusiastic or more interested in yourself than in your conversation partner if you speak too much.

➢ Maintain a positive mindset

We show self-control by being joyful during a talk.

People are also more likely to want to chat to someone who is upbeat rather than someone who is constantly complaining.

➢ Use the FORD method.

The FORD method defines an acronym that provides us with conversation topics. It's an abbreviation for Family, Occupation, Recreation, and Dreams.

If you remember this word, you'll always have at least four relevant conversation topics.

➢ Plan ahead of time for certain topics.

Prepare some conversation topics ahead of time. Topics for specific circumstances, such as exchanges with coworkers, managers, or lifetime friends, may be planned. If you prepare ahead of time, you won't be caught off guard with nothing to say.

PROFESSIONAL WAY OF COMMUNICATION

Communication is the transmission and reception of information using various spoken and nonverbal strategies. Communication skills are required while giving a presentation at work, brainstorming with colleagues, discussing a problem with your boss, or checking project details with a client. They are an important part of making strong professional contacts. While it may seem that communication consists mostly of talking and listening, there i0s much more to it. Everything from your face expression to your tone of voice influences communication. We'll look at what communication skills look like at work and how you may improve them to become a more effective communicator in this piece.

The four different types of communication

Your communication talents will be divided into four categories. Let's go a little further into each of these topics.

➤ Written communication

Writing is an older mode of communication. We often write as part of our job, connecting via email and messaging systems like Slack, as well as in more formal publications like project reports and white papers.

Written communication necessitates communicating information in a clear, simple, and appropriate tone of speech.

➤ Verbal communication

Many of us communicate verbally in the workplace to impart information. This might be anything as informal as discussing an impending deliverable with coworkers, or something more formal like meeting with your manager to examine your performance.

Listening closely to what others are saying is also an important component of verbal communication.

> ➤ Communication that is not verbal

Body language, eye contact, and overall attitude may all be used to send nonverbal messages to others. Nonverbal communication abilities may be improved by using appropriate facial expressions, nodding, and keeping eye contact. To successfully convey a message, verbal communication and body language must be in sync.

> ➤ Nonverbal communication is the fourth mode of communication.

Finally, visual communication refers to the use of images, graphs, charts, and other non-written communication strategies. Visual aids are often used to enhance or replace textual material. In any case, make sure your visuals are clear and serve to reinforce your message.

What is the importance of communication abilities?

We use communication skills in our work lives in a variety of ways, including talks, emails and written papers, presentations, and visuals such as graphics or charts. Communication skills are vital in the workplace since they allow you to:

1. Enhance your interactions with your employer and coworkers.

2. Develop connections with your customers.

3. Assist you in conveying your point as quickly and clearly as possible.

4. Improve your professional appearance.

5. Encourage active listening and inquisitiveness.

6. Assist in your professional progression

Building safety relationships

What are the BSA's most critical provisions?

The BSA is a difficult and wide piece of legislation made up of six components, some of which have yet to be fully implemented. Certain portions, such as the BSA's landlord and tenant obligations, are outside the scope of this article; nonetheless, several important aspects are included below.

The Authority for Building Safety

The BSA established the building Safety Regulator (the regulator), an independent entity tasked with overseeing the new high-rise residential building regulatory regime. Part 2 of the BSA covers provisions concerning the regulator's role. According to the BSA, the regulator's functions must be carried out in order to guarantee the safety of people in or around buildings from hazards presented by structures and to improve building quality. The regulator must also examine transparency, accountability, proportionality, and consistency.

Buildings that provide a greater danger

The implementation of building control regulations for higher-risk buildings (HRBs) is one of the regulator's most critical duties. In terms of design and construction, a building is regarded more dangerous if it is at least 18 meters tall and has at least seven floors. Nursing homes and hospitals are also included in this category. Occupied buildings, on the other hand, are only more dangerous if they additionally include at least two residential units. Nursing homes and hospitals are not included in the latter idea.

As the building control authority for HRBs, the regulator is responsible for inspecting HRBs during construction and registering new and existing HRBs. The deadline for registering existing HRBs has already passed, with the regulator recently stating that over 13,000 duty bearers had started or finished their applications to register ahead of the October 1, 2023 deadline. New HRBs must also be registered with the authorities prior to occupation.

The claim limitation time has been extended.
The most well recognized provisions of the BSA are modifications to the Defective Premises Act 1972 (the DPA). Notably, the BSA extends the limitation period for claims arising under Section 1 of the DPA (the duty to create suitably residential structures) to 30 years retrospectively (before June 28, 2022) and 15 years prospectively (after June 28, 2022). Furthermore, the BSA adds a new Section 2A of the DPA requiring anyone working on a building containing a house to guarantee that such structures are fit for habitation when finished. Similarly, the limitation period for claims under Section 2A of the DPA is 15 years.

Individuals who are accountable and have responsibilities

Part 4 of the BSA creates the 'accountable person,' who is legally responsible for the safety of inhabited HRBs and is obliged to study building safety concerns and report to the regulator on an ongoing basis. The responsible party might be the landlord or freeholder of the building, or the entity in responsibility of repairing common spaces.

While the accountable person is responsible for inhabited HRBs, the BSA also creates new duty holders who are legally responsible for the work done on HRBs as well as the appointment of those offering construction services. Duty bearers include clients, main designers and individuals with design duties, lead contractors, and all contractors participating in a project.

What impact will the BSA have on the construction industry?
This is the central difficulty for construction professionals negotiating the BSA's intricacies, and it is a wonderful example of how regulatory change and commercial motives often coexist. While the BSA's long-term impact is uncertain, some potential repercussions may be suggested.

The claims landscape is shifting.
Changes to the DPA, such as a lengthier limitation period, have opened up new options

for litigation against those responsible for poor work. For example, new owners of a property inside a building may now submit a claim for improper construction under Section 2A of the DPA. It remains to be seen if the DPA amendments will increase the number of claims; nonetheless, construction professionals must be mindful of the BSA's emerging claims environment and seek to manage any potential risk correctly.

Construction contracts

Construction lawyers will very probably be talking with their clients whether key elements of their suite of construction contracts should be rewritten to conform to the new climate. They may, for example, try to address changes to the limitation periods in the DPA and reallocate project team roles in compliance with the BSA's new duty holder scheme. However, it should be noted that the updated drafting to account for BSA standards has yet to be tested, and it is uncertain how the courts would interpret it.

Education and training

Since the founding of the BSA, the construction industry has prioritized education and training, illustrating the impact of significant regulatory change on any business. Construction professionals and duty holders must stay current on the BSA's evolving building safety regulations, as well as any relevant secondary legislation, in order to remain in compliance.

One area that is likely to be the subject of ongoing training is the new 'golden thread' of building safety information, which must now be electronically stored in compliance with the BSA throughout the duration of a facility. Indeed, since the accountable person is responsible for retaining a 'golden thread' of information for both older and newer HRBs, the availability of relevant information is likely to be crucial in terms of compliance with the new storage and reporting obligations.

As is usual with large-scale regulatory reforms, the full impact of the BSA may take years to become obvious. On the one hand, the BSA may present new hazards for construction professionals to deal with, but on the other hand, it may inspire more accountability and transparency in the sector, which is consistent with Dame Judith Hackitt's goal of rebuilding public trust in the building safety regime.

Misunderstandings of others' actual sentiments

Some people find it difficult to express their feelings, which may lead to misunderstandings and hurdles in interpersonal interactions. Here are some critical thoughts to overcome this issue:

Recognize and Accept Emotions

Recognizing and accepting one's feelings is one hurdle. Encourage people to self-reflect and become aware of their emotions, resulting in a better knowledge of their emotional condition.

Increase Emotional Vocabulary

Some individuals have difficulty expressing their feelings in words. Suggest that they practice extending their emotional vocabulary so that they can express their emotions with more accuracy and clarity.

Make Use of Descriptive Language

When describing feelings, emphasize the necessity of utilizing descriptive language. Instead of broad remarks, urge people to become particular, resulting in a more realistic reflection of their sentiments.

Investigate Creative Outlets

Those who find it difficult to communicate their feelings orally can consider pursuing creative avenues such as painting, writing, or music. These media may function as additional outlets for emotional expression.

Practice in Low-Stakes Environments

Overcoming the problem of expressing emotions often needs practice. To gradually gain confidence, start with low-stakes scenarios and communicate sentiments in a controlled atmosphere.

Seek Relationships of Support

Encourage them to seek out supportive connections where they may express their feelings without fear of being judged. Trusting relationships may provide a secure area for emotional expression.

Make use of "I" statements

Teach the usage of "I" phrases to assertively communicate feelings. Framing sentiments with "I feel" instead of accusatory comments fosters personal accountability and clarity in communication.

Investigate the Root Causes

Addressing trouble expressing emotions may need investigating the underlying issues. Encourage people to look into prior events or ideas that may be impacting their capacity to express themselves honestly.

Tips for Making a Great First Impression

Making a great first impression is critical for both personal and professional success. Here are some ideas for making a strong and pleasant first impression:

- Pose and confidence

Maintain proper posture and radiate confidence while standing tall. A confident posture may instantly draw attention and express self-assurance.

- Eye Contact and a Smile

A genuine grin and eye contact may quickly establish a relationship. They exude warmth, approachability, and genuineness.

- Strong Handshake

A strong, but not obnoxious, handshake conveys strength and confidence. Maintain eye contact when shaking hands for maximum effect.

- Appropriate Dress

Appropriate attire for the event conveys professionalism and respect. Take note of the dress requirements and strive for professional, well-groomed clothes.

- Listening Actively

Actively listen by nodding, keeping eye contact, and answering properly. This demonstrates that you regard and respect the individual with whom you are conversing.

- Consider Your Body Language

Pay attention to your body language. Open and pleasant gestures, such as uncrossed arms, indicate openness and receptivity.

- Clearly introduce yourself

Make an effort to introduce oneself properly and convincingly. Speak slowly and clearly, making sure your words are heard and well-articulated.

- Make Your Elevator Pitch Memorable

Prepare a succinct and convincing elevator pitch. Clearly describe who you are, what you do, and what sets you unique so that the audience remembers you.

- Discover Common Ground:

Look for shared interests or experiences to bring up throughout the chat. Shared ties foster rapport and familiarity.

- Demonstrate Genuine Interest:

Inquire thoughtfully and show real interest in the other person. This shows that you appreciate them and are actively participating in the relationship.

- Keep Time in Mind:

Be timely and manage the length of your contact correctly to respect the other person's time. Avoid taking over the discussion.

Remember the following names

- Attempt to memorize and utilize people's names. This personal touch communicates attention and respect.

Send Follow-Up Emails:

- Following the first encounter, send a follow-up note expressing appreciation and reinforcing your desire to keep in touch. This extends the pleasant impression beyond the first meeting.

Create Your Own Personal Brand:

- Create a distinct personal brand that embodies your beliefs, talents, and personality. Your personal brand's consistency improves recognition and memorability.

How to Make Meaningful and Long-Lasting Connections

Making significant and long-lasting connections requires a mix of genuine interest, good communication, and a dedication to fostering relationships. Here are some tips to help you make long-lasting connections:

Authenticity is essential:
- Be real and sincere in your dealings. People value honesty, and authenticity establishes the basis for trust in every connection.
-

Discover Common Ground:
- Determine common interests, values, or objectives. Common ground serves as a firm basis for connection and aids in the formation of a feeling of camaraderie.
-

Communication that is open:
- Communicate in an open and transparent manner. Honest and transparent communication fosters confidence and

helps in the prevention of misunderstandings.

Reciprocity:
- Promote reciprocity by giving and getting in equal proportion. This might involve providing assistance, giving thoughts, or just being available to others when they need it.

Empathy and comprehension:
- Practice empathy by seeing yourself in the shoes of others. Understanding their points of view and feelings enhances and strengthens partnerships.

Success should be celebrated:
- Recognize and applaud the accomplishments and victories of others around you. This indicates your genuine concern for their well-being and achievements.

Be Consistent and Reliable:
- Establish trust by being dependable and consistent. Keep your promises and be reliable, since this builds trust in your relationships.

Using Positive Reinforcement:
- Offer encouragement and positive reinforcement. A cheerful and encouraging atmosphere promotes well-being and develops relationships.

Shared Experiential Learning:
- Whenever feasible, create shared experiences. Whether it's working on a project together or experiencing unforgettable moments, shared experiences strengthen relationships between people.

Respect Individual Differences:
- Understand and accept individual diversity. Accept and value the various

traits that each individual offers to the partnership.

Show Your Appreciation:
- Express thankfulness for the contributions and presence of persons in your life on a regular basis. A simple "thank you" may go a long way toward fostering strong relationships.

Adaptability:
- Be adaptive and open to new experiences. Adapting to changing situations enhances your resilience and, as a result, your relationships.

Invest Time and Energy:
- Making long-lasting friendships takes time and effort. Devote the resources required to cultivate and sustain your connections.

Accept and Forgive:

- When problems develop, be prepared to apologize and exercise forgiveness. Addressing and resolving disagreements helps to strengthen ties.

Keep in Touch:
- Staying connected in our fast-paced world takes work. Check in with folks in your network on a regular basis, whether via face-to-face meetings, phone conversations, or virtual contact.

Suggestions for Social Gatherings

Attending social gatherings may be both exhilarating and difficult, particularly for individuals who want to improve their interpersonal skills and general well-being. Here are some self-help ideas for social situations:

Set reasonable expectations:
- Approach social gatherings with reasonable expectations. It's not necessary for every contact to be significant, and it's OK if you don't connect with everyone.

Use Positive Self-Talk:
- Encourage a good mentality by using positive self-talk. Replace negative self-talk with affirmations that increase your confidence and self-esteem.

Start Conversations:
- Be the first to strike up a discussion. Introduce yourself, ask open-ended questions, and demonstrate genuine interest in people.

Body Language Is Important:
- Be aware of your body language. To generate a friendly presence, maintain open and inviting postures, make eye contact, and smile.

Quality trumps quantity:
- Prioritize the quality of interactions above the number. It is more vital to make genuine relationships than to meet as many people as possible.

Control Social Anxiety:
- To handle anxiousness and be present in the moment, use relaxation methods, deep breathing, or mindfulness activities if you suffer from social anxiety.

Learn and Recall Names:
- Attempt to learn and recall people's names. Using names in talks shows attention and develops bonds.

Discover Common Ground:
- Look for subjects or shared interests to discuss. Finding common ground aids in the development of rapport and makes interactions more pleasurable for both sides.

Transitions in Mindful Conversation:
- Smoothly transition between subjects in chats. Take note of indicators that indicate interest or indifference and alter your themes appropriately.

Compliments and gratitude:
-   Thank them for the chance to communicate with them, and don't be afraid to express honest compliments. Positive feedback fosters a happy environment.

Invite a Friend:
-   Attend social activities with a pal if feasible. A familiar face may provide comfort and ease to social encounters.

Set realistic time constraints:
-   If attending social activities drains your energy, establish realistic time restrictions. It is OK to take pauses and recharge when necessary.

Be True to Yourself:
-   Value genuineness. Being real and true to oneself builds stronger ties.

After-Event Analysis:

- After the event, consider your social contacts. Consider what went well and what you might do better in the future, seeing each encounter as a learning opportunity.

Additional Information:
- Build relationships by following up with individuals you meet. Send a thank-you note or indicate interest in future conversations to demonstrate your appreciation for the friendship.

16 methods for obtaining topics to discuss

Creating intriguing and engaging subjects to discuss may improve your discussions and make social interactions more pleasurable. Here are some ideas for discussion starters.

Current Affairs:
- Stay up to date on current happenings, both worldwide and locally. Discussing current events, trends, or news is a relevant and timely starting point.

Shared Experiential Learning:
- Discuss mutual experiences or activities to find common ground. These subjects may create connection, whether it's a recent movie, a pastime, or a shared interest.

Pose Wide-Open Questions:
- In order to promote meaningful interactions, ask open-ended questions. Instead of yes/no questions, use questions that elicit thorough replies and encourage debate.

Travel Adventures:
- Discuss or ask about your trip experiences. Discussing various cultures, favorite places, or travel experiences often leads to lively discussions.

Books, movies, and television shows:
- Talk about recent books, movies, or TV series you've loved. This might reveal personal preferences and inspire intense debates.

Aspirations and goals:
- Discuss your aims and desires, as well as those of others. Discussing future intentions might uncover similar goals and spark a nice conversation.

Hobbies and interests include:
- Find out about each other's hobbies and interests. Sports, art, music, and other activities may all spark heated and joyful discussions.

Funny stories:
- Tell entertaining tales or share your own experiences. Humor is an excellent technique to lift spirits and create a good ambiance.

 Technology and devices:
- Talk about the most recent technology advances or fascinating devices. Many individuals like discussing new technology and its influence on numerous facets of life.

Life Lessons and Thoughts:
- Share your life lessons or comments with others. Discussing your life experiences may lead to meaningful discussions and a better understanding of one another.

Popular Culture:
- Investigate pop culture subjects such as celebrity news, viral memes, and current events. These topics are often relevant and may spark lively debate.

Culinary and Food Experiences:
- Talk about your favorite cuisine, culinary experiences, or cooking techniques. Food is a universal issue that typically elicits excitement and fond recollections.

Nature and the Great Outdoors:
- Discuss nature, outdoor activities, or environmental issues. Hiking, gardening, and environmental sustainability are all topics that might spark interesting discussions.

Personal accomplishments:
- Discuss recent personal triumphs or achievements. Celebrating your accomplishments promotes happiness and encourages others to join in your satisfaction.

Philosophical Issues:
- Ask philosophical questions or engage in thought-provoking discussions. Conversations regarding deeper concepts may lead to intriguing intellectual conversations.

Topics for Education:
- Investigate educational subjects or offer fascinating information. Learning together may be a rewarding and enjoyable experience.

How to walk and speak like a star

Walking and talking like a superstar frequently require a blend of self-assurance, composure, and good communication abilities. Here are some pointers to help you project a celebrity-like aura:

How to Walk Like a Celebrity:

Pose with Confidence:
- Maintain a self-assured and erect stance. Walk with purpose, standing tall and shoulders back. Body language that is confident may project a powerful and positive impression.

Movements that are smooth and controlled:
- Make sure your motions are smooth and controlled. Avoid hurried or chaotic movements and move with elegance. Celebrities have a purposeful and polished stride.

Make eye contact:

- Make eye contact with your surroundings. It conveys confidence and demonstrates that you are there and attentive.

Smile:

- Smiling should be sincere and natural. A cheerful disposition and a warm grin may make you accessible.

Appearance: well-groomed

- Take care of your looks. Dress comfortably and stylishly, and make sure your general grooming is on point.

Walking Speed with Intention:

- Walk at a steady yet comfortable pace. Instead of hurrying, which might communicate anxiousness, walk with purpose.

Take Charge of Your Environment:

- Move about as if you own the environment around you. Your gestures may convey an air of power and refinement.

Walking from heel to toe:

- Walk heel-to-toe to achieve a smooth and beautiful stride. This method is often connected with elegance and poise.

Speaking Like a Star

Articulation is clear:

- Use clear articulation while speaking. Enunciate your words to ensure that your message is comprehended.

Tone of Confidence:

- Use your voice to convey confidence. Speak in a steady and controlled tone, avoiding abrupt changes that may imply doubt.

Take Your Time:

- Maintain control of your talking tempo. Avoid speaking too rapidly, and allow your words enough time. Celebrities often talk at a methodical pace.

Intonation Variation:

- Vary your intonation to make your conversation more interesting. A voice with a range of highs and lows may bring appeal to your message.

Listening Actively:

- During talks, be an engaged listener. Respond intelligently and genuinely interested in what others have to say.

Body Language that is Positive:

- Use positive and open body language to accompany your words. To underline points and communicate passion, use gestures.

Gratitude and politeness:

- Be courteous and show thanks. Celebrities often demonstrate humility and appreciation in their encounters.

Keep Up to Date:

- Be up to date with current events and important issues. This enables you to participate meaningfully and confidently to discussions

Humor:

- When appropriate, use humor. A well-timed joke or light-hearted remark might help you become more relatable.

Authenticity:

- Communicate in a real manner. When celebrities speak from the heart and remain true to themselves, they typically connect with viewers.

Effective Advance English Communication

To successfully communicate in advanced English, you must refine your language abilities, including vocabulary, pronunciation, and general communication tactics. Here are some pointers to help you improve your advanced English speaking skills:

Language and Vocabulary

Increase Your Vocabulary:
- Expand your vocabulary on a regular basis. Read extensively in English, including literature, essays, and news, and develop a list of unusual terms.

Discover Idiomatic Expressions:
- Learn to use idiomatic terms and colloquialisms. These enliven your language and make it seem more genuine.

Make use of synonyms and antonyms:
- Use synonyms and antonyms to avoid using repetitious terminology. This demonstrates a more comprehensive mastery of the language.

Learn Phrasal Verbs:
- In English, phrasal verbs are prevalent. To sound more fluid and natural, learn and practice utilizing them correctly.

Make Use of Complex Sentence Structures:
- Practice building difficult sentences. To communicate subtle thoughts, a range of language patterns, including compound and complicated phrases, are used.

Articulation and Pronunciation:

Pay Close Attention:
- Actively listen to native speakers, whether in films, podcasts, or in person. Take note of their pronunciation, intonation, and rhythm.

Regularly practice speaking:
- Consistent practice is essential. Conversations with native speakers or other learners might help you gain confidence and improve your pronunciation.

Capture Yourself:
- Record yourself speaking and listen for places where you might improve. Take note of your pronunciation, tempo, and clarity.

Pay Special Attention to Stress and Intonation:
- Recognize English stress and intonation patterns. This involves emphasizing the proper syllables and incorporating suitable rises and falls into your voice.

Communication Techniques:

Explain and clarify:
- Experiment with clarifying and paraphrasing. If you're not sure about anything, ask for clarification and repeat your words to guarantee comprehension.

Participate in Debates and Discussions:
- Take part in debates or discussions on a variety of themes. This allows you to express yourself effectively and reply to opposing points of view.

Be Aware of Cultural Differences:
- Be mindful of cultural differences in English communication. Understand how to utilize official and casual language appropriately, as well as gestures and body language.

Improve Your Critical Thinking Skills:
- Develop critical thinking abilities. Advanced English requires not just the use of complicated vocabulary, but also the expression of well-thought-out ideas and arguments.

Make Use of Transitional Phrases:
- Use transitional phrases to connect concepts logically. This improves the flow of your speech and allows your listeners to follow your train of thought.

Adjust Your Language to the Audience:
- Tailor your words to your intended audience. Adapt your words and tone depending on whether you're speaking to coworkers, friends, or in a professional situation.

Real-life instances of guidance and tales

Increase Your Vocabulary:
- *Example:* Emily, a voracious reader, sought to broaden her horizons by reading across genres. Reading ancient books introduced her to complicated vocabulary, which made her talks more fascinating and intelligent.

Discover Idiomatic Expressions:
- *Story:* James, an English student, routinely watched English movies. He used the term "hit the hay" to imply going to bed one day. His buddies were startled, and this novel term quickly became a joyful addition to his linguistic repertoire.

Learn Phrasal Verbs:

- *Example:* Maria went to an English language meetup and learnt the phrasal verb "break down." Soon after, she confidently used it in a business meeting to describe a hard idea, impressing her colleagues with her advanced language abilities.

Regularly practice speaking:
- Story: Carlos became a member of a discussion group where he met fluent English speakers. Regular encounters not only increased his confidence but also improved his pronunciation and fluency, allowing him to speak English more fluently.

Capture Yourself:
- As an example, Sarah videotaped herself reading a difficult chapter from a book. She saw areas for improvement after listening, such as fine-tuning her pronunciation of specific phrases and altering her tempo for more clarity.

Pay Special Attention to Stress and Intonation:

- *tory: Alex, a language student, imitated a podcast host's intonation patterns. This exercise improved his capacity to communicate emotions and emphasis in his speech, resulting in more dynamic talks.

Explain and clarify:
- Example: During a business meeting, Mark requested clarification on a technical word from a colleague. Mark's openness to request explanation, rather than just nodding along, established a common understanding, avoiding any misunderstandings.

Participate in Debates and Discussions:
- Story: Rebecca joined a debating group and explored a variety of societal concerns. Participating in these discussions not only improved her language abilities, but also taught her how to explain her arguments convincingly.

Be Aware of Cultural Differences:
- Example: Daniel learnt to handle cultural subtleties in communication while working in an

international team. He discovered that adopting professional language in emails and respecting personal space during talks helped to create a pleasant work atmosphere.

Adjust Your Language to the Audience: Michelle, a language lover, took part in both official and casual language exchange activities. Adapting her language to varied contexts not only increased her adaptability, but also expanded her interactions with a variety of individuals.

.

Acceptance of Thoughts and Emotions:

Acceptance of thoughts and emotions is a basic part of mindfulness and well-being. It entails accepting and letting your ideas and emotions without judgment. Here is a more in-depth look at this practice:

Understanding Acceptance: Acceptance does not imply that you approve or agree with everything you believe or feel. Instead, it is about accepting that thoughts and emotions are a normal aspect of the human experience. Non-Judgmental Awareness: Practice noticing your thoughts and feelings without labeling them as 'good' or 'bad.' Instead, then condemning yourself for specific emotions, practice nonjudgmental awareness. Mindful Observation: Develop mindfulness by examining your thoughts and emotions objectively. This detached observation keeps you from being embroiled in the intensity of the moment.

Avoiding Suppression: Acceptance does not imply suppressing or pushing aside painful ideas and feelings. It's just the contrary - it's about allowing things to come to the surface, recognizing their existence, and accepting that they, too, will pass.

Self-Compassion: - Be kind to oneself. Understand that everyone has a spectrum of ideas and feelings, and you are not alone in this. Speak to yourself with the same courtesy you would provide to a friend.

Radical Acceptance: Practice radical acceptance, a notion from dialectical behavior therapy (DBT). This entails totally accepting the truth of a situation, even if it is unpleasant, and letting go of the desire to oppose it.

Mind-Body Connection: Take note of how your body reacts to various ideas and feelings. Physical experiences are often associated with your mental state. Being conscious of this link adds to a comprehensive acceptance practice.

Breath Awareness: When faced with difficult thoughts or emotions, pay attention to your breathing. Focusing on your breath may help you stay in the present moment and offer a buffer against overpowering emotions.

Labeling ideas: Label your ideas without connection. Instead of expressing, "I am anxious," add, "I am experiencing the thought of anxiety." This verbal change builds distance and lowers connection with the feeling.

Mindfulness Meditation: Incorporate mindfulness meditation into your daily practice. Observe thoughts and emotions as they occur during meditation and let them to pass without becoming caught up in them. Over time, this builds your acceptance muscle.

thankfulness Practice: Develop a thankfulness practice. When troubling thoughts arise, counteract them by meditating on areas of your life for which you are glad. This might alter your outlook and promote acceptance.

therapy treatment: Seek therapy treatment if you find it difficult to manage your thoughts and feelings. Professional assistance may give tools and techniques targeted to your specific circumstance.

Mindful Activities: - Engage in activities that bring you into the present moment, such as painting, music, or nature excursions. By switching your mind, engaging in these activities promotes a feeling of acceptance.

Mantras or Affirmations: Use positive mantras or affirmations to foster acceptance. Repeat sentences that connect with you, establishing a mentality of understanding and loving your ideas and feelings.

Journaling: Keep a diary to express and explore your ideas and feelings. Writing may be a therapeutic technique to examine your experiences and create acceptance.

Decisive Mind Trick

It's crucial to remember that using the word "mind control" in the context of influencing others might generate ethical difficulties. Influence should always be used with respect, honesty, and care for the well-being of others. Instead of concentrating on "mind control," consider how establishing a decisive and persuasive mentality might improve your capacity to influence others: You may favorably influence people and create cooperation and mutual understanding if you develop a decisive attitude that includes confidence, empathy, effective communication, and ethical concerns. Remember that true influence is founded on trust, respect, and the pursuit of mutual objectives.

- Purpose Clarity: - A decisive mind is focused on its goal. Define your aims and objectives clearly, and understand how influencing people matches with common interests and values.

- Confidence and Conviction: Confidence is a vital component of influence. A determined intellect expresses confidence and conviction in its thoughts. When you believe in what you're saying, people are more inclined to listen.

- Effective Communication: Improve your communication abilities. Clarify your opinions and ideas, and actively listen to others. Effective communication is a strong instrument for influencing choices.

- Empathy and Understanding: Develop empathy to comprehend the viewpoints and needs of others. A decisive mind evaluates the problems and motives of people it wishes to influence, laying the groundwork for successful persuasion.

- Strategic Thinking: Consider how your suggestions match with the aims and priorities of your audience. Present your ideas in a manner that illustrates their worth and importance.

- Adaptability: A decided mind is adaptive. Be open to feedback and prepared to adapt your strategy depending on the answers and requirements of the people you're attempting to impact.

- Establish Credibility: Establish credibility by regularly delivering on your commitments and exhibiting knowledge in your profession. Credibility increases your impact and makes people more willing to trust your judgments.

- Positive Influence: Use your influence for good. Seek win-win results that benefit both you and others you are attempting to influence. This promotes trust and long-term connections.

- Persuasive Storytelling: Master the skill of persuasive storytelling. Create emotional connections with your audience, making your ideas more remembered and appealing.

- Conflict Resolution abilities: Develop good conflict resolution abilities. A determined thinker can negotiate issues tactfully, converting potential confrontations into chances for cooperation.

- Lead by Example: Set a good example for others to follow. Demonstrate the behaviors and attitudes you want to see in others, and create a good effect via your actions.

- Respect and Integrity: Maintain a high level of integrity and treat people with respect. A determined thinker understands the value of ethical influence and establishes trust via honest and straightforward communication.

- Patience and perseverance: Influence typically requires patience and perseverance. A decisive mind remains devoted to its goals, modifying its method as required while retaining a long-term vision.

- Continuous Learning: Maintain your curiosity and commitment to lifelong learning. A decisive mind attempts to grasp changing viewpoints and modifies its persuasive methods appropriately.

Conclusion

Throughout this book, we have delved into the complex interplay between words and emotions, which is essential for successful communication. Communicating well with others is an art that requires mastery of several skills, such as reading body language and learning to listen actively. As we wrap up our investigation, let's think about the important things we've learned that will help us handle people well.

The value of empathy, or the capacity to put oneself in another person's position and see things from their point of view, is the first thing we've discovered. Building connection and understanding in our talks, empathy is the foundation of successful communication. It goes beyond mere words, into the domain of emotions and bridging the gap between souls.

The value of attentive listening is immeasurable. Listening attentively has the power to change lives in a society where everyone wants to be heard. It's not enough to only express yourself; we've learned that listening attentively to the complex web of emotions and ideas that others bring to the table is essential to good communication.

The power of non-verbal communication has also played a vital part in our journey. Understanding the silent language of gestures, facial emotions, and posture empowers us with an extra layer of communication skill. Mastery of these details helps us to connect with depth and honesty, beyond the limits of words alone.

In the digital era, we've found the obstacles and possibilities given by the realm of virtual communication. From video conversations to instant messaging, adjusting our communication style to numerous platforms has become vital. The ability to express authenticity and connection via screens is an art in itself—one that we've investigated and embraced.

As we complete our examination, remember that successful communication is not a destination but a constant path of development and refinement. Each discussion is a chance to use the concepts we've identified, to learn, adapt, and develop lasting relationships.

In the broad tapestry of human contact, our words and deeds are the threads that weave the fabric of our relationships. Let us, then, approach each interaction with purpose and grace, inspired by the knowledge garnered from these pages. May the skill of successful communication be a light, illuminating the route to better relationships, deeper understanding, and a society where words become bridges, not walls.

Thank you for joining me on this adventure. May your every discussion be a beauty of connection and communication.

www.ingramcontent.com/pod-product-compliance
Lightning Source LLC
Chambersburg PA
CBHW070833260726
48660CB00005B/2041